Holiday Rental Law On the Spanish Costas 2013

Robert Grieve Black

© Copyright Robert Grieve Black 2013

Foreword from the author:

I first wrote this little guide in 2012 as "Holiday Rental Law in Catalunya" because this region of Spain (with Barcelona as its capital) was the first to formulate a realistic and workable system of licensing and control for vacation rentals. However all the available information was in Catalan or Spanish so I made this little guide in English. Then the Spanish Government made small but significant changes to housing law in June of 2013 and there was a great hullabaloo in the press about Spain banning holiday rentals, so I did a little more research and republished the guide in August 2013 as "Holiday Rental Law in Spain". It is now the middle of December 2013 and some more information has become available so it is time to republish again. It is one of the great advantages of digital books.

The truth is that for expat property owners and holidaymakers most of the Autonomous regions of Spain are not of great importance. Nearly all of the famous "costas" of Spain lie on the Mediterranean seaboard down to where it meets the Atlantic. That is from the French border with Catalonia down to Seville in the South. Then out to the east of Catalonia are the Balearic Islands and away down level with the south of Morocco lie the Canary Islands.

The Costa del Sol is in the region of Andalucía. The Costa Blanca is in the Valencian Community. The Costa Brava and Costa Dorada are in Catalonia. The Balearics include Mallorca, Ibiza and Menorca while the Canaries include Gran Canaria, Tenerife, Lanzarote, Fuerteventura, La Palma and eight smaller islands. So this guide will concentrate on the current norms and laws in these regions.

The Canary Islands have been restricting holiday rentals for many years. The Balearics were very restrictive for a while but seem to be close to doubling the number of legal villas in the last year or so. Catalonia still appears to be the best region having issued close to 25,000 "licences" in the last year. Valencia is a bit more nit-picky with documents and conditions but it is not obligatory to register. Andalucía, the one that most people are waiting for, is still dragging its heels so we have to second-guess what's going to happen there. Across the board the picture is nowhere near as bleak as the British gutter press are screaming about. Sorry Daily Mail but you are well and truly in that category.

INTRODUCTION.

This little book (one reviewer called it a pamphlet) has been compiled from a variety of sources and is to the best of the author's knowledge correct. However the situation is fluid and the regulations vary from region to region and from town to town. It is the responsibility of each person to verify his or her obligations and the author cannot be held responsible for any misinterpretation.

If you are in any way connected with or interested in the rental of holiday apartments you cannot have missed the hoo-ha of baloney in the press in recent months about the "banning" of private holiday rentals in Spain. It was irresponsible and grossly misleading. If you are the owner of a property in Spain, then yes, 2013 is going to be a turnaround year and you need to get yourself in the loop or you could face enormous fines. Enormous means what it says on the tin; anything up to €90,000 in some places. So it is important that you know what is really happening and that is by no means easy. But it doesn't mean that Armageddon has arrived.

This little book will not tell you everything but hopefully it will point you in the right direction. During the next couple of years there will be very few people who can give you an absolutely clear picture so do not be taken in by the "experts" who claim that they know. Let's make this bit crystal clear. The following people DO NOT KNOW and they will probably have some financial interest in your believing that they do: lawyers, property agents, holiday rental sites, newspapers, travel experts, Spanish gestors, and expat websites. You really will have to get up off your butt and search around yourself. Spain has seventeen autonomous communities and the two main cities also have the right to exercise separate by-laws. Add to that the idiosyncrasies of all the tin-pot generals in the local "ayuntamientos" and you have the perfect recipe for confusion.

In the Telegraph, May 13th this year, Fiona Govan wrote, "SPAIN TO CLAMP DOWN ON HOLIDAY RENTALS," and continued later in the article saying that the Spanish government is "poised" to pass a law that will restrict the right of owners to engage in holiday-lettings. This type of sensationalist reporting is inaccurate, panic-mongering and in lots of ways unhelpful. It is unhelpful to a government that is making real efforts to eliminate the black market economy and it is unhelpful to owners who need some real facts and advice on what they will have to do. Above all it is misleading and unhelpful to the millions of holidaymakers who need to be able to book their accommodation with confidence. People need to know when changes take place but most news articles are sensational rather than informative. The Spanish Government has not banned and doesn't really plan to ban private holiday rentals. The intention is to bring some order, legality and security to an extremely fragmented industry. After all if you were a holidaymaker renting a holiday home in another country, would you not want to be sure that it really exists, that it meets basic standards, that it is insured and that you have somebody on site to contact when there is a problem?

These days everybody gets their information from Google but take care. So much of the bumph that floats around is out of date and most of the information you find still relates to professional agencies and holiday complexes and not to private renters. To get information that relates to your property try googling your own town name followed by *"vivienda de uso turistico 2013"*. You have to include the year because there is so much still out there that refers to days gone by and even this is no guarantee that the information is correct. You will have to check and double check. Or better still go to the Town Hall (ayuntamiento) and find out first hand.

THE NEW LAW

This was the new law that received so much publicity. It did not even hint at banning holiday rentals. In fact it did not specifically deal with holiday rentals. It was all about improving the flexibility in the residential property market. But there was one miniscule little clause that threw the holiday rental market into disarray.

Ley 4/2013, de 4 de junio, de medidas de flexibilización y fomento del mercado del alquiler de viviendas.

Law 4/2013, June 4th. Measures to foment flexibility and movement in the rented housing market.

This new law incorporated revised conditions in the rental contract for permanent housing. The minimum contract was reduced from five to three years. The tenant is no longer bound to the contract for its duration and can opt out after six months. The owner now has the right to reclaim the dwelling for personal use. The two parties are now free to decide the annual increase in the rent; previously it was linked to the national price index.

As with most laws there were various appendices and amendments. There will now be a new national register of people who have been evicted by the courts for non-payment of rent. And tucked away in Amendment 1.5, Article 5e we find that six short lines have thrown the apartment rental world into a state of panic and confusion.

Ammendment 1.5 Article 5e.

Por último, en los últimos años se viene produciendo un aumento cada vez más significativo del uso del alojamiento privado para el turismo, que podría estar dando cobertura a situaciones de intrusismo y competencia desleal, que van en contra de la calidad de los destinos turísticos; de ahí que la reforma de la Ley propuesta los excluya específicamente para que queden regulados por la normativa sectorial específica o, en su defecto, se les aplique el régimen de los arrendamientos de temporada, que no sufre modificación.

Translation: Finally, in recent years there has been an increasingly significant use of private accommodations for tourism which may be creating situations of intrusion and unfair competition, adversely affecting the quality of tourist destinations; hence the proposed law reform specifically excludes them so that they are regulated by specific sector rules or, failing that, they apply the regime of seasonal leases, which is not amended.

(Author's notes: 1. By excluding holiday rental properties from the basic housing laws it effectively removes the freedom that owners have had for many years to escape the controls and taxation imposed on other types of holiday accommodation. 2. "Seasonal lease" means that a family rents your apartment or house for the whole of the summer season. This used to be a very common practice and it has returned to some extent in the last few years due to the difficulty in getting a mortgage for a second residence. The price paid is usually less than what you can earn with weekly rentals but it is a very real option for anyone who does not want to get involved in any new registration process. The biggest advantage is that you don't need to provide a 24 hour contact number.

So this little clause did not prohibit holiday rentals. It simply stated that we can no longer rent a property for just one week under the same umbrella of legislation as permanent family rentals.)

This means that for most regions of Spain, holiday rental properties went into a state of limbo. They have not been made illegal but they were eliminated from one set of rules before the new set were in place. In this book you will find a predominance of detail on Catalonia. That is because Catalonia introduced a very good framework of holiday rental law before the National government abdicated the responsibility.

SO WHAT IS REALLY HAPPENING?

The principal is fairly logical and certainly not complex. Spain had four main categories of dwelling or lodging: hotels, camp-sites, tourist apartments and domestic dwellings. There was and still is a clear distinction between an apartment in a holiday complex and an apartment in a residential complex. The tourist apartment blocks were clearly defined and were an integral part of the Spanish tourist industry. The current problems have been caused by the exponential growth in the use of residential houses and apartments for tourist use. A massive new market sector has grown in the last ten years of private apartments and villas being offered to tourists direct from the owner. The Americans have dubbed this FRBO (for rent by owner). It is not only Spain that has seen the need to control this market. France, Italy and Greece have quite stringent controls. The City of New York rocked the boat recently by declaring that the rental of private dwellings to tourists is prohibited by city law.

Spain is perhaps unique in the sheer volume of private dwellings that are owned as second or third residences or simply for speculation. There are, in addition, thousands of unsold properties in the Costas. In the five years since the economic crisis began to bite the market has been flooded with properties for holiday letting.

The different categories:

Tourist Apartments: These are called *Apartamentos Turisticos* in Spanish and it is extremely improbable that you own one of these. They are blocks of apartments dedicated entirely to holiday rental and usually have one owner or a syndicate of owners. You tend to find these in tour operators brochures. They have been specially designed for the purpose. You cannot have a normal apartment registered in this category.

Domestic Dwellings: These are called *viviendas* in Spanish and are private houses and apartments. This might be a villa on the hillside or a small one-bedroom apartment in one of the coastal resorts or an apartment in the centre of one of the cities. (It is crucially important that we differentiate between apartments and villas.

Casas Rurales:

This is a category of country house in small villages which operate a type of bed-and-breakfast. You cannot have a bed-and-breakfast business in a town of more than 2,500 inhabitants.

What is happening now is that a new category has been created called **Vivienda de Uso Turistico.** In Catalunya it is called **Habitatge d'Us Turistic**. This category is for normal apartments, town houses and villas that were previously classed as *viviendas* but are currently used for holiday rentals. There are two very clear reasons why this has been done. Firstly, the long term private renting sector was in need of revision. The Government wanted to update the laws on long-term property letting to give more flexibility in the protection of both tenant and landlord. They also wanted to augment the number of rentals on offer while at the same time to encourage promoters to bring unsold properties into the rental market. It was impossible to impose binding contracts of significant duration when the law permitted rentals of a week or even a few days. Holiday rentals needed to be taken out of the housing equation to enable solid contracts and conditions to take effect. Secondly, we have seen this virtual explosion of the holiday rental market in internet in the last ten years. Spain is struggling to control its infamous black economy and these holiday rentals have been without any form of monitoring or control. However the solution has been somewhat ill-planned. Central government has really just passed the buck to the regions. In June this year they slipped a small clause into their new law on home rentals that says in effect that any private dwelling used for holiday lets is now excluded from the residential sector. This does not mean that they have put a ban on the activity but it has put many thousands of owners into a virtual state of limbo. The law does not say holiday rentals are illegal. It says that they are no longer covered by the umbrella of the laws on residential housing. Each autonomous region must absorb this sector into its legal framework as it pertains to tourism, not to housing.

There are three additional factors that have received a lot of press in the last couple of years. The associations of Hotel owners and of the owners of blocks of tourist apartments have been vociferous in their demands that the government do something about the anomalies that existed. These sectors have to abide by various fiscal and legal restrictions while this massive, ever-growing, clandestine sector is free to operate with impunity. Also some residents' associations complained bitterly about the disruption caused by uncontrolled groups of tourists in residential accommodation. Meanwhile several activist groups claim that the use of private dwellings for tourist use removes otherwise vacant accommodation from the housing pool creating an imbalance that shrinks the supply for people seeking permanent rented accommodation. Private owners, on the other hand, protest that the property is rightfully theirs and that they should be allowed to do what they want with it. Alas, this is a luxury that is diminishing fast in the modern world. Every facet of life is subject to some form of law and order. Those of us with a touch of realism recognise that the under-the-counter free-for-all of the last twenty years could not continue. Honest, respectable owners welcome the changes provided they are administered orderly and fairly.

The holidaymakers who rent this type of accommodation seldom feature in the crossfire of whether or not new legislation is needed. But at the end of the day they are likely to benefit greatly from the creation of some form of registration and control. Unfortunately there is little doubt that the inevitable taxes and administrative costs will push prices up. Exactly how much, nobody knows. However there can be little question that these changes will ultimately benefit families or individuals seeking to rent holiday accommodation. We must be moving to a point, maybe two years hence, where the big online rental sites are only carrying legally registered properties. In the meantime they have all jumped on the bandwagon of signing deals with agencies. Spanish agencies are more crooked that individual owners. Just because a property is listed by an agent does not mean it is legal. It is of paramount importance that the big players accept their legal and moral obligations. After all to build a secure, authorised, legal selection of properties must make economic sense too. Credibility is a key factor in marketing.

Anyway, this new category has been created by default and the Spanish central government has passed the control of this new "sector" to the autonomous regions. It is simple. It is logical. It is no big mystery. However the law has been changed quickly and the regional authorities are not fully prepared (and with the financial crisis they don't have funds) so nobody really knows what is going to happen in any of the seventeen communities. The exceptions are: The Canary Islands who have had controls in place for many years, The Balearics who have had a licensing system for a number of years (but still have about 40% unregistered) and Catalunya who introduced their own new laws last year. The Catalans are a pragmatic people and have set in motion a reasonably workable system of registration. It took a full year to get off the ground and there are still a great many owners who have not registered but the Province of Girona (the Costa Brava) now has almost 4000 legally registered properties. It seems likely that most of the other Communities will copy the Catalan model. We have spoken about the hoo-ha of publicity about bans and fines and other doom and gloom stories so it is worthy of note that the town of Lloret de Mar initiated legal proceedings this summer (2013) against fifty-six owners who have not complied with the new Catalan laws.

In the meantime, probably up to late Spring or early summer of 2014 and in most regions of Spain, the activity of holiday rentals will not be covered by any law whatsoever. As new laws are passed in each of the regions there will be a state of flux while the situation eventually becomes more stable. In the meantime most owners will probably choose to muddle through. There really is no other way. If you don't know where you are going, any road will take you there. People can be prepared and vigilant and can help one another along the road. Keep pestering your local town hall. Go to the tourist office, not the public office that hands out maps. Find your way upstairs to the planners. Every town council has a *"regidor de turismo"*. He or she may not be very knowledgeable or helpful but if enough people push and shove the constant drip will eventually wear away the stone and there will be some movement. Pick up the little free newspapers in the street. They are often surprisingly informative. Try to read the Spanish national newspapers and if you aren't too hot on the lingo just pop the text into the Google translator. If you have paid adverts in the big websites, then pester them to death about the current situation. They have an obligation to inform their customers or the legal situation. Keep a written note of all your attempts to get information. Keep all your email. Keep this little book to waggle in front of the judges' noses. If you can prove that you tried to be legal it may stand you in good stead if you are unlucky enough to be prosecuted through ignorance.

WHAT WILL BE THE NEW LAW ON HOLIDAY RENTALS? WHAT FORM WILL IT TAKE?

Man is a strange creature. He hates change and yet he insists on changing everything. But truth be told, the situation regarding holiday rental properties in Spain was in desperate need of change. Nobody knows exactly how many properties were on offer for rent nor to what extent each owner was successful. However there have been several independent studies researching tourists on arrival and it became blindingly obvious that an enormous sector was in existence without any form of regulation. One estimate puts the size of the market at €2000 million per year. Almost none of this income was declared and in many cases was paid to home owners from abroad in their own countries. In many small coastal towns throughout the Spanish Mediterranean coast this black market of accommodation outstripped the official legal supply of hotel places. In addition many of these apartments were situated in buildings where most were first-residence or second-residence of Spanish citizens.

Up to 2012 the law was very basic in its application to this type of rental. In short you could do what you wanted but in theory were obliged to declare any income from this source. As previously noted, both the Canary Islands and the Balearics had restrictions in place but the rest of Spain was a free for all. However several new laws have been passed across Spain that are directed at long term renting in order to give more protection to both tenant and landlord. These new laws, as we have seen, were impractical for rentals of one or two weeks. The autonomous region of Catalunya pre-empted the situation and passed a new law in 2011 that became effective at the end of last year. In June this year in the latest of these new law changes, the Government of Rajoy removed holiday rentals totally from under the umbrella of protection of private dwellings for the whole of the Spanish territories.

There has been a strong lobby of Hotel Owners pressing the Government for change over the last five years. Private holiday apartments form a distinctly different market to Hotels and the competition they offer to the hotel sector is minimal but it is fundamentally wrong that one sector should be subject to control while another be totally free of any type of regulation. Although this lobby was motivated by self interest one of their lesser arguments was that the free for all in the self catering sector provided practically no protection for the consumer. There was no guarantee of the quality of any property nor indeed, that it even existed. Quite a number of well-publicised frauds have been perpetrated whereby fictitious properties were advertised and potential renters unwittingly fleeced of their holiday money. Just a simple register of holiday homes can eliminate much of this type of fraud.

So, although there will be regional and local variations the basic list of controls is likely to be as follows:

Firstly a register of properties with individual registration numbers.
Some form of control of the quality of each property.
A requirement to have permanent 24-hour contact in the case of problems.
A register of the people renting the property.
Some form of guarantee that income is declared for tax purposes.
Notification to neighbours and other owners that you are conducting this business.
Perhaps some form of taxation commensurate with the VAT that is charged in other accommodation types.
Participation in tourist tax in the regions where it applies for other types of accommodation.

Third party insurance cover.

If you look at each of these factors individually most observers would agree that they are reasonable and indeed necessary. These are in fact the basic ingredients of the new Catalan system although for the moment they have not imposed any new taxation. It is a sensible, workable system and so it seems very likely that the Catalan system will be adopted or adapted by the regions around the coasts while some of the cities will want to impose more stringent controls prohibiting holiday lets in certain parts of the city. This has happened in Barcelona and is already being talked about in Madrid.

Nearly every autonomous region will incorporate all or most of the above controls. The main difference will be in the documentation you have to produce. Some will follow the Catalan example and permit the rental of both villas and individual apartments. Some will follow the example of the Balearics and restrict apartment rentals to the tourist apartment complexes.

THE NEW LAW IN CATALUNYA (CATALONIA)

Substantial changes were made in 2011 and 2012 affecting the legality of renting out a house or flat in Catalunya. They really were several giant steps ahead of the Spanish central government. The Generalitat (Catalan Government) conducted a major review of the laws affecting property ownership and property letting in order to clarify the rights of the owner and of the individual renter. They also updated the laws affecting tourist accommodation especially with regard to registering with the Department of Tourism. Then they found that a great swathe of private properties were being rented out to holiday makers and that this was not covered by the laws on property letting nor by the laws on tourism. The new law on "Habitatge d'Us Turistic" was in effect a bridge between the two previously classified areas of law. The Spanish government, in June this year, just took this "great swathe of private properties" and dumped them in a vacuum outside the ambit of the law. The Catalan government, two years before this, identified the problem and made specific new regional laws to encompass these properties. In lots of ways we in Catalunya are lucky that we already have the new system in place.

So how does the Catalan system work? Number one, every property that is advertised for rental to holidaymakers must first be registered with the Department of Tourism of Catalunya. Fines are possible of up to €90,000 for non-compliance. While it was obvious that there would have to be some leniency during the transitional period, the authorities set 29 September 2012 as the closing date for registration of properties that were currently being advertised in internet or were with agents. As well as this register you have to set up an account with the Mossos d'Esquadra (police) in their register of "viatgers" the same as hotels have to do, and you must notify each let along with the names, identity or passport number etc. of each person in your property. And of course all rental income has to be declared. Although it wasn't clear in the initial presentation it soon became clear that we would also have to collect tourist tax. This is an irritation rather than a financial burden. The tax is not high.

The new laws were assembled as part of a programme called Omnibus which set out to make it easier for owners to come within a framework of legality. It now plugs the gaps that previously existed and eliminates most of the grey area that allowed thousands of properties to be rented out in a clandestine manner. The new system applies to all property owners whether they are Spanish nationals, foreigners with Spanish residence or nationals of another country who do not reside in Spain. It applies whether you rent out the property directly or through an agency. It is the owner who is obliged to register.

In Catalunya it is not something that is "going to happen". It has already happened and everybody who has been renting out any type of dwelling must register it as a "habitatge d'us turistic". The biggest problem for non-Catalan owners is that information is still sparse and what you do find is all in Catalan. All of the documentation you will require is in Catalan. You will not find much help from an estate agent or lawyer or gestor because, although this has been in the pipeline for a couple of years, they have been hit by surprise too and are largely clueless. Even the people in the various town halls (who have the responsibility of doing the registration) did not really know how to handle the situation. They had been sitting on their thumbs hoping it would all go away and now the Generalitat have saddled them squarely with the task.

Catalunya is something of a paradox. The present day government "Generalitat" is modern thinking and outward looking. They have spent a lot of time studying, consulting and revamping many areas of the law to make it applicable in the 21st century. Just twenty-five years ago it wasn't obligatory to have your house in the property register. Now there are substantial controls and guarantees that work towards protecting the individual citizen. All land and property whether residential, commercial, industrial or agricultural must be inscribed in the local property register and in the provincial cadastral register. The paradox, however is that these changes meet with enormous resistance from the Catalans themselves. If it's working why fix it? They don't mount street demonstrations or anything like that; they just ignore the new laws and bury their heads in the sand until they realise that the change is inevitable and then embrace it with great fervour. This recalcitrance of the local people could, in fact, work in your favour. If you act now you can get ahead of the crowd.

So what do you need to do? How do you go about it? Where do you have to go? What documents do you need? Do you have to pay? When must you do it? Are there any options to avoid this? Should you stop advertising your property? Who can help you? What are the implications for the renters?

BASIC REQUIREMENTS

OK. So this is what you have to do if your property is in Catalunya.

All owners of holiday rental properties in Catalunya must apply for a licence for each property that they propose to rent out to holidaymakers. Up till now only commercial entities have needed to register with the Tourist Department. That is to say all hotels and pensions, all youth hostels, all campsites, all aparthotels and blocks of holiday apartments, all agencies representing owners. As of 2012 all holiday accommodation must be registered with the Tourist Department either in Barcelona, Girona, Lleida or Tarragona. The vehicle for this registration is the local tourist office which is part of the "ajuntament" in each municipality. The government of Catalunya, the Generalitat, said that all properties must be registered by the 29th of September 2012. However neither the local town halls nor the Generalitat itself were properly organised or integrated for the task. Nevertheless the law has been passed and ignorance is never accepted as an excuse for non-compliance with the law. In essence this move is not very different to the registration of bed and breakfast establishments in the UK. It is a move to bring a large uncontrolled sector under the wing of governance.

It may seem perverse to some people that Spain is now insisting that holiday rentals are registered but not long term letting, while in the UK it is a criminal offence to rent property long term without a local authority licence but not for holiday rentals.

In any case, all owners must register via their local town hall using a document called "Comunicacio Previa d'Inici d'Activitats d'Habitatge d'Us Turistic" which means "first notification of intention to use a dwelling for holiday rentals". There is a standard model of this document and you can find it to download as a PDF in internet but most Ajuntaments like to have their own headed documents. Along with this application form you have to provide the following:

The easy one to obtain is the last receipt for the payment of your local taxes. This is called IBI or "Impuesto sobre Bienes Inmuebles" in Spanish or "Impost sobre Bens Immobles" in Catalan. If you pay it by direct debit the bank will be able to give you a copy. If you can't find it go to "Recaptacio" in the town hall and they will give you proof that it is paid. If it isn't paid you need to pay it and get the receipt.

The second document that is absolutely essential is the "Cedula de Habitabilidad" (habitabilitat in Catalan). This is a small slip of paper about the size of an envelope that confirms your property is officially habitable and it also gives the maximum number of persons who can occupy the property. There is a chapter of this book with a full description of the CEDULA.

The third thing you need is not really a document but you must have complete details. You need to have 24-hour telephone access for your renters in the case of breakdowns and other emergencies. This has to be a person or an agency that is permanently in the vicinity. In some cases, if you are resident here during the summer season it can be you, but in general most towns may insist on a local professional service. Most towns have a couple of multi-service agencies of the type that are used by insurance companies for 24-hour emergency call-out. You need to provide the name, address, identity number, phone number and email of this person or agency.

The fourth requirement is that you must have somebody who can represent you to the Catalan authorities and who will ensure that all the administration is in order. It can be yourself but you need to be able to complete the documentation in Catalan. Most people recruit the services of a "gestor" for this type of documentation. For this you need the same details as for the 24 call-out service. It may be that this person presents the application for you, in which case you and your representative both have to sign the document. There are also some ex-pats who offer this service.

The town of Lloret de Mar is also asking for a photo of the front elevation "fachada" of the building and is asking that you certify that the other owners in the building have not blocked tourist use. The most recent version of the law tried to strip out as many niggles as possible in order to get the registration process moving but some towns will inevitably introduce their own variations. If the community of owners in any particular block of flats have voted to stop holiday rentals this has to be done by a Notary and written into the statutes of the community in the property register of the town. If you are not up to date with the history of your apartment block you may have to visit the local "Registre de Propietat" to check. Or if your community has a good administrator they will have a copy of the statutes.

When you have all of these things you can begin the process of registration either in person or with the help of a representative. The document as we said is "Comunicacio Previa d'Inici d'Activitats d'Habitatge Turistic." If you type these words into Google you should get a model of the document. Also as we have said some "ajuntaments" or town halls have their own headed document. They are now quite organised and will give you a copy to complete which you should return in duplicate with a photocopy of the IBI and CEDULA (and photo of the building if required). The standard procedure for everything in Catalunya is that you present the document to the "Registre" in the reception area of the town hall. They will check it is in order and you must make sure they stamp your copy as proof that you have presented it. It should also get an entry number. Some towns may insist that you present the document to the Tourist Office. That is the administrative office, not the girl you ask for a map.

One of the things you have to agree is that the property will be adequately insured but there does not seem to be any requirement to produce evidence of this.

The Town Hall is obliged to take your presentation provided it is all in order and they will check the residential zoning status of your property before passing your documents to the Department of Tourism of Catalunya in Girona or Barcelona or one of the other offices in Lleida or Tarragona. Then you just have to wait while the wheels turn.

If you own a holiday rental property and are still not registered, it is extremely important that you get started NOW. Do not delay. If you can show that you have set the thing in motion it is very unlikely that you will be prosecuted. We should all already have this done but it was the administration who dragged their heels. Now the system is fully integrated and there is no excuse for not complying. Some legal proceedings have been initiated in some towns.

THE RESIDENTIAL STATUS OF YOUR PROPERTY

In Catalunya, as in the rest of Spain, real estate properties are classified into several categories. A house or flat that was built or adapted for habitation is called a "habitatge" (vivienda in Spanish) and if you rent it out it is a "habitage d'us turistic". A block of apartments that was built specially for holiday rental purposes like an Aparthotel or a complex that is all under the same owner is called "apartaments turistics. There is one anomaly that exists in Catalunya more than in other regions with regard to this type of property. At the height of the property boom some of these were divided into separate apartments and sold off but they remain classified as tourist apartments not dwellings. If you have bought one of these apartments that were originally aparthotel you will have real problems because you cannot get a "cedula de habitabilitat". If you are planning to rent out a private detached house this is the least complicated type of dwelling but may be affected by the zone it is in (see below). If you own a villa that is divided in two it is very unlikely that permission was granted for two dwellings and you will have to get two individual cedulas. The next category is commercial property usually called a "local". If you have a local that was adapted to a dwelling without full permission you will not get permission to use it for holiday rentals. The final group of properties is the illegal developments. If there is any discrepancy in the official status of your property your application will be blocked.

There are two other areas where your application might hit the buffers in the initial stages.

Each town hall has its own plan of land development and if your house or apartment is in a purely residential zone it may not be accepted. This could be the case, for example, in townships like Castell Platja d'Aro, Calonge, Pals, Estartit/Toroella, and Palafrugell or Reus where the main town is set back from the beach and the strip along the beach is considered touristic and the main town residential. At the time of writing it is still not clear how this will all pan out but it seems likely that zoning will play a part in the granting of licences especially as they reach high numbers.

The other important aspect of the new law is that the Comunitat de Propietaris ("comunidad de propietarios") in a block of apartments can vote to disallow holiday rentals in their block. However this may not be as ominous as it sounds. In order to make this change it must be written into the statutes of the community. It must be presented in the order of the day at a full meeting of the community and it requires that 80% vote for the change. This 80% means four fifths of the coefficients of floor area so that the owners of bigger flats have a bigger vote. The City of Barcelona adopted the new law very quickly and in some parts of the city it is now impossible to get a licence. Many neighbours objected to the groups of hen-party/stag-party people that have flooded into the city in recent years thanks to low-cost flights. In order to check this you need to see a copy of the statutes of the complex. This is a legal document that is inscribed in the Property Register of the town. You may be able to obtain a copy from the administrator of your block

*Once more the author seeks to emphasise that all of this information has been accumulated from fragments drawn from various sources. It is the responsibility of every owner to verify the situation as it applies to him or her.

TAXES

It is fairly obvious that one of the prime motivations in this new set up is to enable the government to collect more taxes. This is in fact perfectly correct and normal in a modern democratic state. If we earn money from any source it is supposed to be declared. If you have a business or a work contract and you are already declaring tax you will not find this a big difficulty. If not, you need to find a "gestor" or "assessor" who will do your tax documents for you. You can offset the level of tax that you pay by keeping a record of all the costs involved.

Your house or apartment is considered to be in the category of "habitatge" or dwelling and renting out a dwelling does not incur VAT (IVA) so you will not have to do a declaration of "IVA". This may change in the future since the Spanish law in June has now excluded holiday rental properties from the habitatge/vivienda category. As things stand now (September 2013) if you provide cleaning services or babysitting or get over-involved in providing linen and towels and welcome packs your business can be considered "hostaleria" like a hotel and you in theory you would be eligible to charge VAT and do a declaration. However this would involve a completely different application with many more complications.

Catalunya has a tourist tax. For the year of 2013 it was forty-five cents per adult up to a maximum of seven nights. So for a family of two parents and two kids staying a week or more the tourist tax was six Euros and 30 cents. It is not a lot but it is a pain in the butt for the owner. You have to collect the tax and invoice it. You may decide to include it in your rental price but the law says you have to invoice it. Then you have to do a quarterly return for each property that you own.

For now you do not have to charge IVA (VAT) nor do any declaration. There is of course VAT charged by the online advertising sites and online booking sites and by local agents and administrators. You cannot reclaim this VAT but when you declare your earnings you can deduct all legitimate costs including any VAT that you have paid. It is important that you keep records and receipts for everything that you spend in relation to the rentals. Now that the national government has removed the protective umbrella of "vivienda" classification the door is open for VAT or some new type of tax.

In all cases you have to do an annual tax return and declare the income (less costs) that you have earned. This is not new; it's just that with the transparency of registration it is not possible now to be clandestine. Most people use a local "gestor" or "assessor" for this tax declaration. But be very wary of these "professionals" who offer their services online; you could end up paying more that necessary.

THE CEDULA DE HABITABILIDAD

What on earth is this? In fact it is a very simple form of certification to prove that your property is an authentic, approved dwelling. In essence it is very similar to the Home Report that was introduced in the UK to accompany house sales except here it is a permanent, renewable document that is required for buying, selling, renting and for utility contracts.

If your property is less than fifteen years old you will already have a current cedula so get searching. You can obtain a copy but it's complicated. It is called "Cedula de Habitabilidad de Nueva Ocupacion". It is issued when the new construction receives approval for completion and that it is ready for occupation. This document is valid for 15 years.

If your property is more than 15 years old and you bought it in the last year or so it will probably have a renewal cedula. It is called "Cedula de Habitabilidad de Segundo Mano". Check inside the "escritura" or "copia simple" that you got from the Notary at the time of purchase. In a separate part of the law on "habitatges" it was decreed that a "cedula" is now required for all sales or rental contracts or to sign up for the utilities of gas, electricity and water. So even if you are not going to do holiday rentals this is an essential document to have.

If your property is more that 15 years old and you bought it a few years ago you will not have a current Cedula and you need to get one now. You have to find an "Aparellador" or in Spanish "Aparejador" sometimes called "Arquitect Tecnic". This person is like a cross between a surveyor and draughtsman and he (or she) will come to your property to measure and examine it to see if it complies with regulations. He may tell you that you need a dividing door on a toilet or ventilation for the escape of gas. He may tell you that you need more power points. He may insist on more major alterations.

He will ask for a copy of your IBI (local tax receipt) so that he can find the number in the Catastral Register. If your property was not properly registered it will not be in the "catastro" and he will not be able to do the cedula.

When he has completed the inspection he will either tell you what you need to fix if it is minor or he will ask you to put things right and he will come back. He will also tell you if he thinks your property has problems that will prevent the issue of a Cedula. If he agrees to go ahead he will send the papers to the Generalitat and you will get the cedula about six weeks later. You may get a random inspection from the Generalitat.

Quite apart from holiday rentals it is essential that you have a CEDULA. As explained above you cannot sell your house without it.

A word of warning! You will find several companies online who offer to do an instant cedula at a reasonable price. Remember the cost is in two parts; one for the services of the surveyor and another for the "tramite" or delivery of the documents. The total cost is about €150 euros. The online companies offer it for about €80 plus twenty or thirty euros for the "tramite". It really is highly recommended that you use a surveyor who has local knowledge. You can find one easily in yellow pages or you can ask your bank. The "aparellador" is the person who does the valuation for a mortgage so the banks know all the local people.

In this process of registering your property for holiday rentals in most towns this "cedula" is likely to be your only outlay but you need it anyway.

The Certificado de Eficiencia Energetica.

What's this one all about? This is another new law that came into effect in summer 2013. If you put your property up for sale or for rental you must have this new certificate. What about holiday rentals? Each person must satisfy themselves as to how it applies to their case but it appears that short term rentals are exempt. If a property is rented out for less than a quarter of any year the certificate is not required. For places like Costa Brava where the season is short most owners should be OK. Down south where the season is much longer owners will have to be able to prove their case. In any case this requirement is a separate issue that is not at the moment involved in the granting of permission for holiday rentals. It is mentioned here because it is a real factor in the overall picture. But you must check your own position and not rely on the author's interpretation.

ALTERNATIVES TO HOLIDAY RENTING

Under the definition of "Habitatge d'Us Turistic" in the new law it is a house or apartment that is rented to another party for financial gain for periods of 31 days or less (the original draft of the law said 3 months and it may be that some town halls apply this criterion). But working with the definition of 31 days or less it means that 32 days or more takes the rental contract out of this classification either into short term or long term letting. Other regions may fix this at 60 days or even at 3 months. If you rent to one family for more than this number of days it is a different classification that does not require registration. If you look at the legislation it refers to "seasonal rentals", rentals that take in all of the summer. These are still embraced by the laws on normal housing.

With the strengthening of the law some people may consider that long term renting is now a more attractive option. Long term letting has its own advantages and disadvantages and has to be thoroughly investigated before becoming involved. It involves a contract with conditions that work heavily in favour of the occupant. The income you earn for a year's let will be roughly the same as you can earn from about 8 weeks of summer rental. However, bear in mind that the main surge of demand in this market is coming from immigrant families, many of whom do not have a regular source of income. This applies equally to immigrants and transients from your own country. There are lots of Brits looking for long term lets but check that they have the means to pay. If they don't pay the law is now securely on your side but it is often very slow.

Short term letting is different but still requires that you draw up a contract. There are four distinct areas of opportunity. Firstly with the current instability in the property market many newly arrived ex-pats choose to rent for the first few months till they get a feel for things and at the opposite end there are some people who have sold their home in Spain but want to stay on for a while. The monthly rental rate for this is about double the rate for long term rentals. Secondly if you have an apartment in Girona or Barcelona you may be able to cash in on the student market. Thirdly, but lesser in size, is the market for rental to teachers who are only here for the school session. The fourth possibility lies in a market that was shrinking but has seen a small revival in the last two years. Many families from Barcelona like to spend the summer or a large part of it on the coast. The price for this is about half of what you can earn from weekly rentals but if you don't have a licence it may be the only option. All of these options still require that you declare the income you earn but they are covered by standard housing law and do not require a licence, as is the case for tourist accommodation.

If the property in question is a large villa in a small township you may consider applying for a licence as a "Casa Rural", the Catalan equivalent of bed and breakfast. It must be in a village of less than 1000 inhabitants.

If you are one of these lucky people who has lots of family and friends back home who want to come and rent your property this falls outside the parameters of the new law. You still have a legal obligation to declare any earnings either in Spain or at home but you do not need a licence. The licence is required if you advertise on the internet or in any publication or if you rent through an agency, in essence if it is a commercial venture. And remember, you cannot slip through the net by just advertising in British websites.

Quick resume:

If you advertise your property for short stay holidays in any form whatsoever you must be registered. If you just rent to friends and family you are exempt. If you rent long term you are covered by housing law, not tourist law. If you rent for medium term (from one to six months depending on the location) this is also covered by standard housing law and not the new tourist law. If you rent just rooms in your house this is totally illegal in every case unless you have been granted a licence as a "Casa Rural" in one of the small villages.

RESUME OF WHAT YOU HAVE TO DO (Catalunya)

If you decide that you want to go ahead and have your property listed this is how you have to proceed.

The first thing you have to do is find your "Cedula de Habitabilidad". If your house is more than 15 years old you will probably have to contact a surveyor to come and do a renewal.

The second is to find the receipt for the last payment of local taxes (IBI) or go and pay it.

Then you need a copy of the application document "Comunicacio Previa d'Inici d'Activitats d'Habitatge d'Us Turistic".

Then you need to decide who is going to be your 24 hour call-out service.

Then you need to decide whether your command of Spanish or Catalan is sufficient to complete the application yourself or whether you need professional help.

You also need to check to see if the statutes of your community preclude holiday renting. (This does not apply if you own a detached villa)

Then you complete the form and present it yourself or via your professional helper to your local town hall.

Then you have to just tread water and wait.

If you get a licence you then have to register with the Mossos d'Esquadra and notify each let.

You have to keep an accurate record of visitors and notify the Mossos online.

You will have to keep an account of your revenue and costs and do a yearly tax declaration (Declaracion de Renta).

You could of course just forget the whole thing and hope that Big Brother won't catch you but Spain has changed incredibly in the last twenty years and nowadays that is not a sensible option.

ONE MAN'S EXPERIENCE

I was prompted to write this book to help other people after my own experience in getting off the ground with the new legislation in Catalunya. So perhaps it is appropriate to end this little guide with an outline of my own experiences.

My wife and I have lived on the Costa Brava since 1986 where we have had a small English language school in the town of Palamos. At one point, when we were looking for new premises to rent, I came across an advert in an estate agent's window of an old building with three floors. The price was give-away and our bank was willing to come up with a mortgage. So we got three floors for the same monthly cost as renting premises. We smartened up the top two floors and put an advert in Dalton's Weekly. With the aid of a fax machine we began to get quite healthy summer bookings. Then the same agent offered us an old hostel that had gone to auction. So once again we donned the painter's overalls (and plumber and electrician) and this time got a new school and three large floors to rent out.

About the same time we sold our own house and the other old building, paid off some of the mortgages and then bought three shiny new apartments, a small flat above a bakers and a little house with a garden. With a new batch of mortgages we moved into the first floor above the new school and have been here since 1997.

We had it all beautifully planned; rent out the properties for a few years and then sell everything off for our old-age pension pot. I checked several times across the years with the local tax office who assured me that as long as I declared the income it was perfectly legal and as they were all "viviendas" I was not liable to charge or pay VAT (IVA).

Then of course came the crunch when the banks collapsed. All chance of selling our properties flew out the window. By now we were advertising in the big holiday rental sites in internet and although the season here is only about 6-8 weeks we still managed quite good bookings and we have managed to keep afloat.

At the end of 2011 I was passing by the local cinema and noticed a stand of give-away newspapers in the foyer called Pergami. I took one and read it as I strolled to the post office. An article in Catalan about "habitatges d'us turistic" caught my eye and I was shocked to read that the Generalitat (Catalan Government) was planning to clobber holiday rentals. Over the subsequent months I checked in Google regularly in English, Spanish and Catalan but there was scant information. Then in

June of 2012 I picked up another Pergami and read that we all had till September that year to register our properties or face fines of up to €90,000. The article also pointed out that all properties would require a "cedula de habitabilidad" certificate and that some local councils could well limit both the number and zoning of properties that would be granted a licence. There was also a proviso that owners' communities could group together to decide that their block or complex would not have holiday rentals.

Our three new properties automatically had a cedula de habitabilidad from the builder, valid for fifteen years, but we had four other flats and a house that were older and did not have a cedula. My first move was to visit an ex-student who was now a building surveyor (aparejador) and he came to do the inspections. It cost me about 100 Euros per property and I had to make a few small alterations but within a month I had all of our properties covered. Next step was to do a "Notificacio Previa" at the tourist department of the town halls to set in motion the granting of licences. We have six apartments in the town of Palamos, one in neighbouring Sant Antoni de Calonge and the little house in Platja d'Aro a few miles along the coast. I thought it would be quite straight forward. It wasn't. They were totally clueless about the requirements or the procedure and to a large extent I was telling them what they had to do. I will describe the situation in each of the three municipalities and this will give readers some idea of what lies ahead in the coming year for the rest of Spain.

The closing date to register was the 5th of September 2012. I went to the town hall of Palamos in the second last week of August. I was directed to an elderly woman sitting at an elderly looking desk in an obscure corner of the street lighting department. She gave me a form to complete then shrugged her shoulders and said she had no idea how or when the process would take place. I went back a couple of days later with all the requisite documents and photocopies. I was told I would have to take them to the registry in the main building of the "Ajuntament". They in turn accepted them, stamped one copy with a date of entry for me and informed me dutifully that they had no idea what would happen next. I have to point out at this stage that there was nothing to pay for this registration service. Between August and the following spring I called in to the tourist department several times but they were able to give me absolutely zero information about the process. Everything was in hand I was told and I would get a letter from the tourist department of the Province of Girona. (Although on my last visit

I was told that they still hadn't been sent to Girona). I will return to Palamos later.

Also in August 2012 I took the completed forms to the municipal offices in Calonge for our one apartment there. After a few phone-calls upstairs the receptionist told me I had to go to the public tourist office in Sant Antoni de Calonge and speak to Merixtell. Merixtell was a classmate of one of my sons. She was happy to meet "el Papa de Iain" and with a wonderful smile she assured me that she would look after everything.

Next was the nearby town of Platja d'Aro where we had the little house. I actually found someone there who had some idea what it was all about. He took my papers and checked them off against his list. He escorted me downstairs to the registry to have my copy stamped and I left the office feeling reasonably comfortable that this time they knew about the changes.

So with two applications stamped and dated and carrying a "numero de entrada" plus the platitudes and assurances of Merixtell I felt comfortable that I had at least done my duty. It was abundantly clear in all three cases that I was more or less the first person in each municipality to make an application. But I was happy to have set my licences in motion and confident that for the time being I could go ahead with advertising our properties for the 2013 season.

At the end of September 2012 I got an email from Meritxell inviting me to complete an attached form and bring it to her office. I downloaded the said form to find that it was an application for "apartaments turistics" also called by the abbreviation DRIAT. As I have outlined in previous chapters this classification is for large blocks of tourist apartments with one owner. I phoned her to say that in my opinion she had made a mistake. Oh, no, she assured me. She had been to a big meeting of the Department of Tourism in Girona. This was the correct form. Just fill it in and bring it along. I filled it in and brought it along with a note clipped in front stating clearly that I was applying for "habitatge d'us turistic" not for "apartaments turistics." My application was for HUT not for DRIAT. The receptionist accepted my papers but had absolutely no idea what I was babbling about. How could I possibly know better than them? Next day Meritxell phoned me. "I have sent your application to Girona," she informed me in Spanish. "We didn't use the form you completed yesterday. The first one you brought in August is OK. It is a little different to our form but you have all the documentation correct. If you pass by the office you can pick up the stamped copy of your form". So now I had all three applications officially stamped.

Nothing more happened until January of 2013. I get a phonecall from a clerk in the town hall of Platja d'Aro. My application was ready to send to Girona but I hadn't paid the relevant tax. Whoa! Hold it there! The government proclamation back in June stated that all the town halls had to administer the applications without any charge. Not true he told me. It was a commercial activity and the "ajuntament" had decided that they were imposing a tax on the applications. It was €280 euros but for the first year they were doing a "bonificacio" so I only had to pay €140. I went along to the office and argued my case again but he was adamant that if I wanted the application processed I would have to pay. So why wasn't this all done in September? He just shrugged his shoulders. OK. I agreed to pay.

But it wasn't just that simple. First I had to go to the registry and ask for an "instancia" which is the official document for all requests to the council. I had to request the 50% reduction in the tax then take the form to the accounts department who in turn had to stamp and sign that I was being granted the discount. From there I had to go to the cashier to pay and then back to the lad who had phoned me in the first place. He told me that everybody else had paid and they were just waiting on mine so all the applications would be sent to Girona the following week. I told him indignantly that I was the first person to make an application back in September. Another shrug of the shoulders.

My cheery friend Meritxell sent me a letter at the beginning of February to inform me that my apartment in Sant Antoni de Calonge now had the official number HUTG-000337. So despite her initial laid back approach she was the first to come up with the goods. I looked with interest at the number. I was fairly sure that 337 people had not registered in Calonge but surely it couldn't be the total number of applications for the whole of the Girona Province. Bear in mind that Lloret de Mar and all of the Costa Brava are in the Girona Province. I went to Google and keyed in HUTG-000337 and up popped an obscure department of the Generalitat with an excel document detailing all the numbers to date. I looked for Palamos and found absolutely hee-haw, not even one. I looked for Platja d'Aro and found nothing; then I remembered that the municipality is called Castell Platja d'Aro. I scrolled up to the Cs and was delighted to find HUTG- 000569 for my little house. There were in fact about a thousand properties registered but the Costa Brava must have about a hundred thousand holiday rentals. The

Catalan Government had obviously been super-successful in getting the message out!

I was still worried about my six apartments in Palamos. Why were they taking so long? I went along once more to the tourist desk in the lighting department. Everything was in order the lady assured me. There had been such a lot of applications to deal with. All the papers would be sent to Girona next week. But this is February; all the applications were supposed to be processed by September at the latest. I told her that I needed to know if I had permission as the reservations were starting to come in. Yes. You've guessed it; another shrug of the shoulders.

Easter was in March that year and we already had some bookings. I decided to try and get things moving. I found an email address for the Catalan Department of Tourism in Girona and sent a message asking if they knew anything about why Palamos wasn't in the list. I got a very efficient reply saying that my message had been passed on. Next day I got a message from the department in question telling me that Palamos had not sent any applications. This was impossible. They had to have at least my six! I searched around and found the name and email address of the "regidor de turism" (the councillor with special responsibility". She replied very quickly saying that she had passed my message to the head of the tourist office in Palamos. The head of department then emailed to tell me that there were so many application that the office in Girona had collapsed under the strain. I passed this comment to my contact in Girona. She emailed back within a few hours with a complete list of my HUTG numbers. Surprise! Surprise! I now had six lovely new numbers for my apartments in Palamos.

So I imagine that is how it will be for the next year in the other regions of Spain. Perhaps some of them will be worse. Catalunya had been planning to make changes and the city of Barcelona set their operation in motion a full year ahead of the rest of the region. This time the regions have been dumped with the issue by central government and it could well take two years before the mist clears. In the meantime you will find a lot of confusing and often misleading information in the press and in internet.

What can the ordinary owner do to stay on the right side of the law? There is no doubt that many will opt for "let's just take a chance and do nothing." I seriously do not recommend that option. It will catch up and bite you at some point. Here are my recommendations:

Whether your property is in Catalunya, the Balearics or the Canaries, on the Costa Blanca or the Costa del Sol, get yourself up-to-date with the laws that are now in place that affect your town. Absolutely pester everybody till you get an answer and then double-check that it is right. Most of these regions have their regulations in place that are current and active and sometimes there are heavy penalties for non-compliance.

Start by checking out your "Cedula de Habitabilidad". It is a must for renting or selling a property regardless of whether it is holiday rental or not. If you don't have one, get one. Then what next? If you rent all year round you will need to have a Certificate of Energy Efficiency apart from any tourist rental licence. If you are in one of the regions that has not yet laid out its rules, I suggest you pester everybody you can think of to find out what is happening and, most importantly, keep a log of what you have done and a copy of all correspondence. If you have your property advertised in the big websites like Homeaway, Airbnb, etc. then demand that they inform owners of the situation. They have a moral if not legal obligation to keep you informed. Try some blog sites like Laymyhat.com and Angloinfo and other expat sites. Steer clear of offers from the experts but there are some good morsels from the forum contributors. Keep a note of all your visits and messages. If you are ever singled out for failure to comply you can present the judge with concrete evidence of a sincere effort to be legal. And in the meantime keep renting out your property.

DECEMBER 2013. Latest updates.

Most of the Spanish regions have initiated new draft legislation to encompass private holiday rental accommodation but it is a slow process. Here are some that are available.

THE CANARIES

The situation in the Canary Islands seems to be as clear as the water in Peppa Pig's muddy puddles. However there are several factors that are fairly obvious. Firstly, the laws that apply here are not related to the changes that were made to Spanish law in June of 2013. The laws relating to holiday rentals in the Canaries have been in place from as far back as 1995.

There are, in essence, three categories of property showing a distinction between residential complexes, tourist complexes and private villas.

In residential complexes you cannot legally rent out your property for tourist use nor can you advertise it for such use. You can rent it to friends and family but must declare the income.

If you own a property in a tourist complex you can rent it for tourist use if you have a licence to do so and on the express condition that you use a management agency. You can take bookings yourself but the lets must be managed by an agent.

If you own a villa, you can legally rent it to holidaymakers provided you have a licence but it seems that no new licences have been issued for some time and will not be issued in the foreseeable future. As of January 2011 a number of inspectors have been touring the islands searching out an estimated million beds of illegal or clandestine accommodation and in many cases heavy fines have been imposed. If you are one of the lucky people who has a licence it is still advisable to check that it is fully valid. There appears to be no possibility of becoming legal if you do not already have valid documentation.

It is strongly advised that if you currently have a holiday rental property or are considering buying one in the Canaries, you should seek professional legal advice. There are now regular inspections and if you continue to rent or advertise for rent without a licence you will get a very expensive smack on the wrist.

THE BALEARIC ISLANDS (Mallorca, Menorca, Ibiza)

The most important point about the law in the Balearics is that holiday rentals in private apartments is not permitted in any form. Holiday rentals are permitted in private houses, that is individual villas and semi-detached houses. Apartment rentals are restricted to holiday complexes that were built specifically for this purpose, where the whole complex is owned by one person, company or syndicate. If you own a private individual apartment in a building with other owners, you cannot legally rent it out as tourist accommodation.

With a new law passed in 2012 (La nueva **Ley General Turística de las Islas Baleares)** the Balearic Islands now identifies two types of tourist accommodation: Firstly accommodation that is run as a business and offers touristic services i.e. 'establecimientos de alojamiento de turismo rural' and 'apartamentos turísticos'.

It now also identifies 'Viviendas Turisticas', or private holiday homes, which can be registered and used for holiday rentals (as stated above, apartments are not eligible).

How to register your private holiday home

If you have a privately-owned villa that you would like to register, you should apply for an ETV number (Estancia Turistica en Viviendas) at the offices of the Director General of Tourism. Here you can find out how to apply for your holiday rental licence on the Balearic Islands. The information and application form is only available in Spanish, but we have translated the main details for you below:

Property types that may apply for the ETV:

Detached villas and semi-detached villas.

Who can apply for a licence and what are the requirements?

Individuals or companies who promote a residential home for short-term tourist accommodation. This also includes owners who alternate between using the home as a holiday rental and using it for their own personal use.

Your home should have no more than six bedrooms and offer a maximum of 12 guest spaces. There should be a bathroom for every three guests i.e. you must have at least one bathroom for up to five guests, two bathrooms for six-eight guests, three bathrooms for 9-11 guests and four bathrooms for 12 guest spaces.

Documentation:

Most people will find the paperwork quite cumbersome. Below is an outline of what you need and what you have to do.

Firstly, you will need to fill out both the DRIAT application form (Documento de Responsibilidad de Inicio de Actividad de Turismo) and the ETV Questionnaire and prepare the required documentation. Take all of this with you to the offices of the Director General of Tourism and explain that you wish to register your villa for an ETV number: You will also need to take along floorplans of the property and you'll need your passport or residency document.

You will also need to have a written document detailing: name, address, IDUFIR registration number (Identificador Único de Finca Registral), plot size, location, capacity and square metres of bedrooms, bathrooms, living room, kitchen and terrace, building features: number of units, location, unit identification (garage, summer house) and number of floors in each unit, description of common areas (if applicable)

There is a fee payable for registering your property. A fixed fee of 24.84 € per guest. Example: if your holiday home sleeps eight guests, you will pay 198.72 € to register the property.

Of course, you will also need to declare your holiday rental earnings at the end of the year in the 'Declaración de la Renta' (end of year tax return).

How long does it take to register your home?

From application to receiving your ETV registration number, should take a maximum of six months. During this time you will receive an inspection visit to check that your home complies with all the statutory requirements. Don't worry if you don't hear anything during the process, this is positive!

Where do you apply for the ETV Number?

If your villa is in Mallorca, you have to go to:

Offices in Palma Arena
C. de l'Uruguai, s/n, 07010 Palma,
Illes Balears
Tel: +34 971 178 999

If your villa is in Menorca, you have to go to:

Island Council (Consejo Insular), Tourism Department
Seu del CIM Pl. de la Biosfera
507703 Maó
Tel: +34 971 356 050

If your villa is in Ibiza, you have to go to:

Island Council Tourism Department
Av. de Espanya, 49, 2d floor
07800 Eivissa
Tel: 971 195 433

Massive increase in licences issued:

Despite the cumbersome nature of the registration process many people have registered in the last year. In the 25 years preceding the new legislation there were 2,836 registrations. In the past year there have been 1,647 new licences granted. But bear in mind that this applies only to villas. Private holiday apartments are not granted licences so that anybody operating apartment rentals is doing so illegally. As in the Canaries it is not recommended to continue.

THE VALENCIAN COMMUNITY

It seems that in Valencia owners of private holiday homes have the option to register their home or not. It's not requisite, but there are benefits in doing so and the situation may well change in the next year. There is already some indication that holiday rental websites will only carry properties that have a registration number.

The Valencian legislation is contained in ***DECRETO 92/2009, de 3 de Julio*** and you can find how to apply in the website: *http://www.gva.es/portal/page/portal/inicio/procedimientos?id_proc=14752* Unfortunately, although there is an English language option in the website it does not extend to the details of the application but the basics are outlined below.

Expat owners:

The most significant factor for expat owners is that for Benidorm, Calpe, Torrevieja and all of the Costa Blanca you can legally rent your apartment or villa. You may need to recruit the help of a local agency but would appear that the doom and gloom stories in the British press do not apply to you. If you don't want to register, you don't have to but your property must comply with the same requirements as a registered property and you have to declare the income you earn. It seems that it would be advantageous to register at some point in the near future.

Registering your property

If you do choose to go down the registration route, you will need to make the registration with the Registro General de Empresas, Establecimientos y Profesiones Turísticas de la Comunitat Valenciana (General register of tourist companies, establishments and professionals of the Valencian Community). Registrations are accepted for apartments, studios, villas, chalets, bungalows and other similar properties. Your home will need to meet the technical requirements and standards, as set out within the decree, based on its category i.e. Standard, Primary and Superior.

Once the property is registered, you will need to include the registration number and category type in all advertising and promotion of the property. If you do decide to register your home, you will be entitled to use an accredited agent to manage your property and handle the registration.

Codes for "Vivendas Turisticas" or privately owned holiday rentals in the Valencian Community depend on the province your home is located in:

Valencia VT/Number/V
Alicante VT/Number/A
Castellon VT/Number/CS

If your property is managed by an accredited agent, the code will have EG in front:

Valencia EGVT/Number/V
Alicante EGVT/Number/A
Castellon EGVT/Number/CS

These are the Valencian equivalent of the HUT numbers in Catalonia.

Opting to leave your holiday rental unregistered

You can rent your property out for short-term holiday rentals without registering it but you must state that you have chosen not to commit to the tourism accommodation regulation in Valencia in all your advertising. You will also have the obligation to present your rental earnings in the yearly 'rental' tax declaration and pay the due taxes. It is important to note that while you are not obliged to register, you are obliged to have your property meet the standards laid out in the registration. So it is arguable that registration carries advantages.

The following are the 'basic' standards expected from tourist accommodation:

Access, communal and parking areas
Public entrance. Lift (if the accommodation is situated on the fourth floor upwards). Stairs. Parking is not required at standard level

Installations and services
Heating and sound installation in all areas. Wall power outlets in all rooms and a fuse box. Hot water. Evacuation plan situated at the front door of the accommodation. Emergency telephone list. Information

about local attractions and places of interest

Room Sizes (min. m² space)
Main bedroom including wardrobe 10m
Double bedroom including wardrobe 8m
Single bedroom including wardrobe 8m
Living/dining/kitchen 18m
Living/dining 14m
Kitchen 5m
Bathrooms 4.5m

*Studio apartment (total accommodation space consisting of a living/dining/kitchen
area with separate bathroom) 24m

Rental accommodation should be furnished and equipped appropriately, including:

Cutlery, kitchenware and appliances, bed linen, curtains or blinds on the windows and any other appliances and utensils necessary for a holiday home.

Kitchen appliances
Fridge freezer. Electric grill/griddle. Oven/microwave. Extractor fan and smoke alarm
*The kitchen should be equipped with a minimum of two hob burners when the accommodation has less than four guests and three hob burners plus, when it has four or more guests

You can contact the Generalitat to receive a copy of merged regulatory document: +34 963 986 079 and you can download the registration form. Remember that whether or not you register your property, the obligation to declare your earnings for tax is obligatory.

ASTURIAS

Asturias does not have any of the main "costas". It lies between Coruña and Santander in the north west. But it was one of the first to come up with a new plan and the only one to offer online registration. Here they have decided not to allow private apartments to participate in holiday rentals.

In the Principality of Asturias you can now apply for your holiday rental licence online, or at your local/regional Department of Tourism.

Two types of 'privately owned holiday homes' have been established:

Viviendas Vacacionales: city or coastal properties. It seems that only houses qualify as in the Canaries. Apartments are not included.

Casas de Aldea: privately owned country properties, located in small towns and villages or on non-urbanisable plots and are not considered a local business i.e. a 'Casa Rural'

Holiday Homes - Viviendas vacacionales:

Your home may only be rented as a whole unit (not per room). Your home must be available, at least, during the summer months: June, July, August and September and preferably out of high-season too. You must set a price for your rental. Apartments are not considered 'Viviendas Vacacionales'. You must be able to prove that your home complies with local construction and installation regulations. You must have public liability insurance in place to cover possible damages or guest injuries. Your home will need to fulfil the benchmarks as set out in the Decreto 34/2003 (30 de abril)

What will you need to apply?

Your document of identification, or that of your legal representative. Your property title deeds (Escritura). The documents of constitution of your company, if you have Sociedad Limitada or similar. You will also need a Municipal Opening Licence, which you can apply for at your local town hall. You need a floor-plan (scale 1/100) in which each room is specified with the square metres and labelled bedroom, kitchen, etc. You will need to present the receipt for your public liability insurance. Any other documents you believe can support your application

Where do I apply?

As we have said the whole application can be completed online and once the application is processed, you will be notified by recorded delivery. The Principality of Asturias Tourism Department processes your application and the Department of Economy and Employment completes the application.

If you would prefer to apply in person, you can download the forms and then present them at: Registro General de la Administración del Principado de Asturias.

For a "Vivienda Vacacional" the registration number will be: **VV. (number). AS** This is like the HUT number in Catalonia.

Country Houses - Casas de Aldea

Your country house must comply with all the standards set out in the Decree 143/2002, of the 14th of November, for Casas de Aldeas (Rural Tourism Accommodation).

Your home should be located in a village with a maximum of 500 inhabitants, or on a non-urbanizable plot.

What do you need to apply?

Title Deeds (Escritura) for your property or a rental contract which establishes the availability of the house. Title Deeds of your company - if you have a registered 'sociedad limitada' or similar If you have given power of attorney to a representative, you will need a copy of their NIF (Identification document). You must have a floor-plan showing the interior distribution over each floor and the square metres of each room and its location. You also need an opening licence from the Town Hall

(For the opening licence you will need to produce: A Public liability insurance policy. A document from your local town hall, which states that your property is located in a village with a maximum of 500 inhabitants or on a non-urbanisable plot. Two exterior photos, showing different elevations of the property.)

For a "casa de Aldea" you need to be registered with your local town hall as a resident. (apadronamiento)

Where do I apply?

As with the Vivienda Vacacional the entire process of applying for your Casa del Aldea holiday rental licence in Asturias can be completed online or you can download the documents and then present them at:

Registro General de la Administración del Principado de Asturias
EASMU (Edificio Administrativo de Servicios Múltiples)
C/ Coronel Aranda n°2, planta plaza
33005 Oviedo

To apply online go to: https://sede.asturias.es

For more information visit www.asturias.es or call them directly on +34 985 105 500. Ask to speak to the Tourism Registration Department.

Penalties:

Apologies for the absence of information about penalties in this region. The website provides information about making the application. There does not appear to be any information about fines but they are likely to be similar to other regions.

ANDALUCIA

Here we have the Costa del Sol: Malaga, Marbella, Torremolinos, Fuengirola, Mijas, Puerto Banus, Estepona. The list goes on. This is where so many expats have bought property. And this is where the authorities are still prevaricating.

The organisation Apartur, which is a cooperative body of owners, claims that there are over 8000 apartments in Andalucía that are currently being rented outside of the current laws. This is less than the number in the Costa Brava but there are significantly more British and other European owners in the south.

Why the hesitation? The Andaluz government promised answers before the end of 2013 but they have not been forthcoming. The reason is mainly that the Andaluz government undertook a massive review of legislation in the tourist sector in 2011 coming into effect in 2012. (Ley 13/2011). They laid out the definitions, rules, conditions and documentation for every type of tourist accommodation. However they did not include private holiday rentals because at the time they were still covered by the laws on private residential housing. So when the national government put the small exclusion clause into their legislation in June 2013 they were left with egg on their faces. They must have been aware of what was happening in Catalonia. Perhaps they were just peeved that they had forgotten to include "viviendas de uso turistico" in their new legislation. Some spokespeople said that the designation "apartmentos turisticos" was adequate but it soon became clear that this only referred to the tourist apartment complexes, not to the individually owned apartments that appear in Homeaway, Spain-Holiday, Holidaylettings and other big websites.

But despite the lack of a concise set of rules here in Andalucía, private holiday rentals are not illegal and they have not been banned. The website of Apartur says in Spanish that they are "alegal" not "illegal". Nobody likes the state of limbo but it would appear that owners can continue to advertise their properties in the meantime with the caveat that all income must be declared annually.

In the absence of an official site to recommend, owners will find up-to-date information (such as it is and in Spanish) in www.apartur.es.

In addition if you advertise in www.spain-holiday.com you will find up-to-the-moment reports for each autonomous region as it becomes available. The CEO of this website has established contacts with the ministers responsible in most regions.

HOW DOES ALL THIS AFFECT LARGE WEBSITES?

The large websites like Homeaway, Rentalia, Holidaylettings, Owners-direct, Housetrip, Airbnb and others seem, in the main, to be either ignorant of the law or blatantly ignoring their responsibilities.

These large sites know that this is a huge market. Whether by annual subscription or pay-as-you-go they earn between 5% and 20% of our earnings. This is more than the government receive in taxes.

They really need to get up-to-date and participate more in the moves towards legalisation of this market. They need to do this for the holidaymakers who risk their hard-earned cash. They need to do this for the owners who deserve more support. They need to do this for their own integrity and future survival.

One of the few who has spoken publicly in favour of tighter control is Claus Sorensen, the CEO of Spain-holiday. (http://www.spain-holiday.com/rentalbuzz/ceo-claus-sorensen-speaks-about-holiday-rentals-industry) They are about to add a box to the database asking if the property has a registered number in the regions where it is a prerequisite. This has to be an absolute requirement in all holiday letting sites. The customer can then see at a glance if a property is legal. If they don't do this there will be thousands of families who arrive for their holiday to find that the property has been embargoed by the authorities.

Action is required now and these big sites cannot just say it is the responsibility of individual owners. It is a factor that is fundamental to the whole industry. Several large cities around the world have recently placed severe restrictions on the use of private homes for holiday lets. They obviously feel that the housing is needed for their citizens. But Spain is different; Spain is one of the major tourist destinations in the world and many of its visitors want to stay in a private apartment or villa by choice.

WHERE DOES IT GO FROM HERE?

A note from the author.

All of this process is being undertaken by the usual combination of politicians and civil servants. As time passes and regional and national elections take place priorities will inevitably change. The hotel industry traditionally has a strong voice but some of the bigger holiday rental websites and owner's cooperatives are beginning to interact with government so the situation will remain fluid perhaps for two years. Not all regions and cities will embrace the idea of private holiday rentals. Some will seek to prohibit or at least restrict the activity especially in areas of high demand for residential rental property.

However, the wheel is in spin and if you own or plan to own a house or apartment in any of the Spanish regions it is essential that you keep up to date.

Catalunya is now well into its registration process and has approximately 24,000 properties registered (December 2013) with many more in the pipeline. Costa Dorada area has about 5000, Barcelona about 7,700 and the biggest being Costa Brava/Girona with 10,000. While we may regard the process as painfully slow it is worth remembering that at this time last year there were none registered. It is also worth noting that the vast majority of these properties have been registered by proxy by a local administrating agent. Only a few individuals have gone it alone.

I was firmly of the opinion that other autonomous regions would copy Catalunya and they may still do so but it is not as definite as I first thought and they are certainly not jumping into action. If you have property in any of the regions of Spain and have more up-to-date information, please let me know by email to: robert at costabravarent dot com. Whenever I have solid information I will update this guide until, hopefully, it becomes a comprehensive guide for all of Spain.

Just to finish on a humorous note. Much of the talk about the legislative changes has centred on the exorbitant penalties for non-compliance. In the last week it has been reported that since Barcelona City imposed limits on the number of licences they are being traded for as much as €40,000 and €50,000. So there are definitely some advantages in becoming legal.

If you have found this guide helpful please go the Amazon site and do a review. This is the only real way that other people will find it.

THE AUTHOR

The author of this short guide is Robert Grieve Black. His usual offerings in Kindle books include the crime novel Jammy Dodgers, WW2 romance in Across the Bridge, historic fiction in The Legend of Queen Hynde, and some light reading in Three Short Stories. What is the reason for this digression into more serious matters of economics?

Robert has lived in the area of Palamos, Costa Brava for over twenty-seven years and has watched, over these years, the transition from a free-for-all lack of regulation to a more sophisticated regulated European State. For most of these twenty-seven years he has been involved in some way in holiday renting and is now the owner of several rental properties. He was one of the first to apply for licences in the towns of Palamos, Sant Antoni de Calonge and Platja d'Aro. He is not a legal expert but has a university degree in Economics and Marketing.

He has tried to be as accurate and informative as possible in this guide but emphasises that it is the responsibility of each individual owner to verify what is required for his/her particular property. Additionally he warns that as these are new laws in transition there may be changes along the way. Again it is the responsibility of each person to be familiar with his or her legal obligations especially in relation to the declaration of earned income and to the payment of taxes.

This guide is available as an e-book in Kindle or in print version published in Createspace by Amazon.com and Amazon.co.uk

The content is copyright of the owner but anyone may copy and re-publish extracts of up to three or four pages on condition that the source is mentioned and that readers are informed that this is for guidance only and does not represent legal advice to owners.

www.ingramcontent.com/pod-product-compliance
Lightning Source LLC
Chambersburg PA
CBHW070715180526
45167CB00004B/1478